Essential presentation skills

To Jeff Rodgers, my favourite professor.
He changed my life.

And to Inez, my loving wife.
She changed it, too.

Essential
Presentation
Skills

Elmon E Yoder

Gower

First published in the USA by National Press
Publications, Inc. as *Powerful Presentation Skills*
This edition published by
Gower Publishing Limited
Gower House
Croft Road
Aldershot
Hampshire GU11 3HR
England

British Library Cataloguing in Publication Data
Yoder, Elmon E.
Essential presentation skills
1. Business presentations. 2. Oral communication
I. Title
658.4'52

ISBN 0 566 07827 9 ✓

Printed in Great Britain by Biddles Ltd, Guildford

Contents

1

Excuses for not speaking

Ninety-nine percent of failures come from people who have the habit of making excuses. (George Washington Carver)

A bag of excuses

People can think of more excuses to avoid public speaking than for any other activity. Almost everyone has a desire to be able to speak publicly, but we regard speaking with such fear that we are even afraid to try learning. It can become a habit.

Here are some well-used excuses:

- I get stage fright. (A favourite.)
- I have never done it before.
- I do not know what to talk about.

- I might forget what to say.

- I do not know how to organize my material.

- I might run out of something to say.

- What will I do if they ask questions?

Doing something about it

This book is about dealing with excuses. We will be talking about how to handle them so they will not be problems any more. We will also talk about how to prepare material for your speech and how to develop the skills to present an interesting and informative speech.

Public speaking can also do something for *you*. We are going to talk about that, too.

2

What's in it for me?

The highest reward for toil is not what you get from it, but what you become by it. (John Ruskin)

So you want to become a public speaker. Or at least you are motivated to improve. Otherwise you would not be reading this book. I hope you expand this motivation.

Wishes

Have you ever wished you could stand up and make a good speech? Have you seen others move on to new assignments and better jobs because of their speaking ability? While listening to an unusually inspiring speaker, have you sat out there in the audience with thoughts like this going through your head?

- I would like to be able to speak like that.
- I could be promoted if I could speak better.
- My sales would go up if I could speak better.
- My inability to effectively speak is holding me back.

About being motivated

It is good for you to be strongly motivated to develop speaking skills so you can do better at your job. You owe this to your employer and to yourself. It is also inevitable that if you diligently try to acquire these skills you will do better at work.

But there's more! To paraphrase a common expression, you may ask 'What else is in it for me?'

Plenty. It has to do with expanded motivation. If John Ruskin's idea about toil makes sense, there are even greater benefits. They are not so much about what you get. They are about what you become.

Valuable personal qualities

Your life will be enhanced while you strive to improve your ability to speak. Some important attitudes and habits will change ... for the better.

They will not lie dormant until the day when you 'arrive' at being a good speaker. They will improve as soon as – and as long as – you move forward, towards your speaking goal.

It can change your life!

Here is what can happen to you:

- improved vocabulary;

- better reading and listening habits;

- keener interest in things around you;

- improved ability to think and reason;

- more creative ability;

- better ability to handle criticism;

- becoming a better conversationalist and a more interesting person.

It's exciting. Maybe you have never thought about it quite like that before.

3

Speaker's stage fright

Nothing in life is to be feared. It is only to be understood. (Marie Curie)

The number 1 excuse

The fear of speaker's stage fright has kept more people from learning to speak than all the other causes combined. I have not seen any figures on this, but I'm willing to take bets.

Stage fright is fear – pure and simple. Fear is the most devastating of all human emotions. Man knows no problems like the paralysis of fear. It is the sand in the gears of life.

If we are to cope with stage fright we need to understand it – and respect it. More people fail through fear than ability.

Another thing about the fear of speaking – there may not be as much to be fearful of as you think. Our fears almost always outnumber the dangers.

You are not alone

So you say, 'I get stage fright'. Hey! So do I. Although not like I used to. Everybody gets the jitters, to some extent, at the lectern.

You join the ranks with an army of men and women who at one time in their lives were power-less under its relentless grip. But they overcame their fear of stage fright.

Many prominent people have been completely terrorized by any thought of making a public address. Those who have admitted to stage fright are Winston Churchill, Helen Keller and Abraham Lincoln. The list is long. Even Moses, fearful of the task assigned to him, tried coming up with excuses. They all went on to control it. And they became pretty good speakers, too!

4

The cure

Keep in mind what you have to do when you are afraid.
If you are prepared you will not be fearful. (Dale Carnegie)

Bad fear – good fear

Do not be stopped by fear. Constructive fear is good. It is destructive fear that stops you. The trick is to make your stage fright a constructive type of fear – so it works for you instead of against you.

The worried person sees the problem, but only the problem. The concerned person also sees the problem but uses it to help find a solution.

Faith and destructive fear cannot set up housekeeping together.

A few fleas

The first thing you need to do is to have – and keep having – a healthy respect for stage fright. You will always have some. That is good. Use stage fright to help you.

We find Captain Ahab declaring, just before going after the great white whale, 'I will have no man in my boat who does not fear a whale'.

Golfer Sam Snead once said, 'A few fleas on a dog are good – keeps reminding him he's still a dog'.

Be prepared

The next thing you need to do is to be prepared. Do you recall the motto of the Boy Scouts? It's 'Be prepared' – a great standard for life. It is also the way to make stage fright work for you. The more you sweat while preparing the speech, the less you'll sweat at the lectern.

Stage fright has been called the 'sweat of perfection', indicating the importance of preparation.

Dale Carnegie earned an international reputation as a speech teacher – helping millions of people. Read again what he said about fear and preparation. It works for public speaking – and for living, too.

Keep quiet about it

Now for the last thing. Do not even mention your stage fright around other people. No one is interested! I promise never to bring it up again.

5

How to get started

The longest journey begins with one step. (Confucius)

Get started

The best place to start speaking is at school. But if you have now left school and haven't yet started, it's no big deal. It is never too late to learn.

Get started – take your first step. Now!

Reading about it

There are a number of good books about public speaking. Get several and read them. Each author will emphasize various aspects of speaking in a slightly different way. All will help you. But even after you have read a book, such as this one, you will sooner or later need 'hands-on' experience. You cannot learn to swim only by reading about it. You must jump in and get wet.

Places to receive instruction

Here are some places you can go for help.

Institutes of education

Many colleges offer speech instruction for part-time students, often as evening classes, meeting one to three times a week for the course duration of about three months. Some of them are excellent, some only so-so. If you sign up where instruction is not what it should be, don't stay. Move on and find one you like.

Seminars

Numerous public and private organizations conduct speech seminars taught by a trained staff. They are usually scheduled as one to three days of intensive study. Enrolment is often limited, allowing good teacher-to-student contact. They are an excellent way to get a quick start and to receive motivation for continued training.

Clubs and specialized courses

There are clubs and commercial organizations specializing in speech training. Meetings are usually scheduled in the morning or evening, for the convenience of working people. There are also many local societies for people who want to learn and practise public-speaking skills.

Tapes

Excellent public speaking instructional tapes are available. They are often used as supplementary teaching aids by the organizations mentioned above.

Places where you can start

There are many places where you can begin speaking. They are all around you. They are golden opportunities for you to not only begin but also to continue developing your skill. They can be yours simply by volunteering your time.

Oral reports at your job

Start with any assignment you can get – even the most routine and ordinary. Prepare thoroughly; do a good job. You will be surprised how soon the more important speaking offers come.

Service clubs

Volunteer for committee and officer assignments.

Civic groups

Improve your community involvement and speech skill at the same time.

Political, professional and trade organizations

These groups offer a wide variety of speaking assignments.

Religious organizations

Opportunities involve things such as lay participation in the religious service, teaching and a host of study groups and committees.

Other

Become actively involved in groups such as garden clubs, scouting, PTA, children's sports organizations, stamp clubs, Civil War Round Tables, Save the Whales, etc. The list is endless.

Familiar places

You might want to start where you feel comfortable – around familiar faces. Fine! Do it. But move on to new places as soon as possible.

Don't become caught in a rut!

No one is going to make fun of you. I have never seen an audience snigger or laugh at a speaker who has obviously prepared but who is having a tough time. Most people are sympathetic towards a speaker having unexpected trouble. They will be sitting in their seats silently rooting for you. Especially if they know you have prepared and are giving it your best. The audience will know. You can't fool them!

6

The invitation

The invitation – the great honour. (Unknown)

The question

Receiving an invitation to speak is a distinct honour, but with it comes a responsibility. The first question you should ask yourself is: 'Do I have sufficient time to prepare?'

Preparing a speech takes lots of time. Let no one tell you differently. Depending on the amount of knowledge you already have about the subject, you will need about an hour of preparation for each minute at the lectern.

Saying yes

If you receive an invitation and do have adequate time to prepare, accept it. Don't wait until you are ready. Accept it now – and immediately start preparing.

7

What to talk about

But why should he speak before he has anything to say? (Benjamin Withcote)

Consider people

You need to consider people when deciding what to talk about – the audience and yourself.

You

You should stick to something you care about. It can be about what you already know or are willing to learn. There is absolutely no substitute for knowing your subject. You will find it's a good idea to know more about the subject than you can cover during the speech.

21

Believe in what you say

Avoid topics where you will be making statements of either fact or opinion contrary to what you believe. That's deadly!

The audience

Do you remember the question 'What's in it for me?' The audience is also entitled to ask it. Before you decide what to talk about, discover their wants. What are their interests and needs?

Is there anything special to them about the speaking situation – the date, the place? Find out and incorporate it in your speech. It will add a nice touch.

Is there a sensitive issue that would cause resentment or misunderstanding? If there is, don't talk about it.

The audience and you

Talk about things both of you care about. Many speeches are boring because they answer questions no one is asking.

Time

Stick to things you have time to cover. It is better to talk about something specific than general.

Remember – you should give the people something they can carry away.

The title

Don't spend a lot of time trying to come up with a jazzy title. Who cares? No one is going to remember it!

8

Finding material

When you find it, make a note of it. (Charles Dickens)

It never stops. Be on the constant lookout for new material. It starts before you are invited to speak and doesn't stop until after the speech. Here are some ways to find new material.

Being a better listener

Studies show that the average person speaks about 95 per cent of his comments and writes only 5 per cent. Somebody must be hearing all this. But are they listening?

Most of us have received very little training in

listening – maybe none. Often our listening is disgracefully indifferent and sloppy. Do you suppose we are missing out on something?

Here are a couple of suggestions:

1. *Be selective.* Not everything you hear is worth listening to. Don't waste your time listening to worthless chatter.

2. *Be attentive.* Whenever you hear something worthwhile, listen intently and attentively.

To paraphrase Lord Chesterfield's letter to his son, 'Blockheads listen to what blockheads say'.

Listening is a treasure-trove for finding speech material. Here are some places:

- casual conversation;
- radio and TV;
- civic meetings;
- service clubs;
- places of worship;
- other people's speeches;
- kids.

Being a better reader

There is tremendous power in the printed word. It

has been screened, sifted and has stood the test of time. It's permanent. The biggest source of things for you to say will be from what you read. Reading is one of the speaker's 'tools of the trade'. Develop your reading habits and skills.

Here are some ways:

1. *Learn to read rapidly.* One way is to skim or preview. It gives you a quick, overall view. It helps you decide whether to pass on to something else or go back and pick up important details. This can save you time and improve comprehension of what you read.

2. *Pick a quiet place.* Find a place where you are undisturbed and can concentrate. Effective reading is mental work. The last thing you need is noise or interruptions.

3. *Read something new.* Read beyond your present knowledge. If you read only what you know now your interests will not grow. You grow only when you wrestle with the unfamiliar and partially understood.

4. *Seek out a wide variety of reading material.* You can find an endless variety of literature and written material at libraries, bookstores and your home. Some sources are:

   ● books;

- encyclopaedias;

- newspapers and magazines;

- technical, scientific and trade journals;

- manuals;

- government and legal documents;

- religious writings;

- almanacs.

Getting material from your experiences

Your personal experiences are a valuable source. They often will be the reason you have received the speaking invitation. Your experiences add substance and interest to your speech. Sometimes they will be your main source of material, sometimes you can supplement your talk with things you have heard or read.

Be careful you keep the facts of your experience accurate. Don't confuse your opinions with facts.

The public libraries

Become familiar with them. They contain an inexhaustible supply of material. The nice thing about libraries is that the material is stored in a systematic manner – you can quickly find it. But you must know the system!

Also, get to know your librarians. They are capable and glad to help you. Most librarians have brochures explaining how to find things. Ask for one. It will show you how to use the card catalogues, the reference indexes and many other facilities for your convenience.

The public library will probably also have a map of the place where you are to speak. You'll need it!

Your own library

There are some books that you will use so often you may want to buy them. Here are some:

- *Dictionary.* You will be writing most of your speeches. Use the appropriate word and spell it correctly. If you don't own a dictionary, get one.

- *Thesaurus.* This is a book of synonyms and antonyms. A very useful book. Get one of these, too.

- *Encyclopaedia.* These are published either as a book or a set of books, giving information on subjects arranged in alphabetical order. Some list general knowledge; others concentrate on a particular field.

- *Dictionary of quotations.* These books are sometimes called 'Speaker's Handbooks',

'Stories for Toastmasters', etc. They contain maxims, aphorisms, humorous anecdotes, witty comments, short excerpts from significant literature, etc. They are often compiled by noted editors, writers or speakers. The numerous topics are usually carefully indexed to assist.

● *Almanacs*. These are usually published annually as large paperback books containing statistics on many subjects. They are inexpensive, but contain a great amount of information. If you ever need to know the annual catch of Icelandic cod or the gestation period of the East Indian rhinoceros – this is the book.

Personal notes and file system

Your personal notes can be a valuable source of material. Develop a habit of systematically recording and filing them.

The important thing about making notes is to do it now! Make the note to yourself the moment you hear of it, read about it or when a new idea comes to mind. Unexpected thoughts and ideas are elusive. They can flee from memory as quickly as they are received, and they may never return!

Your notes will do you no good unless you can quickly find them. I suggest you start a note file having a well-planned index system. The standard 5 × 8 in. cards and small, desk-top filing boxes available at office supply stores are well suited for your note file.

Be sure your material is accurate. Verify your sources. Have you transcribed it correctly? You have the right to your opinion, but not a right to be wrong with the facts.

Be sure you express the true intent when you summarize others' statements. Quote exactly when you use a direct quotation. If you modify or paraphrase, say so.

Your credibility as a speaker depends upon the credibility of your material!

9

Putting it together

An intelligent plan is the first step to success. If one does not know where he is going, how can he expect to get there? (J. M. Braude)

Speaking is not writing. Before you start putting your material together, be sure you understand some basic differences between speaking and writing – and between listening and reading. These differences will affect the way you will put your speech together – and the way you will deliver it.

- *Clarity.* Writing is permanent – a sort of congealed communication. The reader can go back and read it again. But the spoken word exists only for the moment. It must be instantly intelligible.

- *Dual communication.* The writer communicates only through the reader's sense of sight. The speaker has access to both the eyes and ears of the audience.

Because of these differences the spoken word:

- is more specific than general;

- is more concrete than abstract;

- is more illustrative and comparative;

- has more contrast and suspense;

- has greater simplicity and rhythm;

- has greater energy and eagerness;

- uses more active voice and personal pronouns;

- is more straightforward and climactic.

Three parts

Some wag once said there are three parts of a speech – the beginning, the end and something in between. Let us consider them in the order they occur.

The introduction

Here we first meet the audience. It's your big chance

to get their interest and set the tone for the rest of
your talk. If ever first impressions are important,
this is the place. Here are some suggestions:

- *Acknowledge the chairperson.* Being invited to
  speak is an honour. It is appropriate to
  express your gratitude – to both the chairperson and the audience. Do it graciously.

- *Pick on yourself.* Sometimes the chairperson,
  when introducing you to the audience, will
  make remarks so flowery that they become
  excessive – to the extent of embarrassment.
  If you try to deflate the comments, be sure
  to stick the pin in yourself, not the chairperson.

- *Acknowledge the audience.* The audience will
  appreciate it if they know you are interested
  in them. Now is a good time to weave into
  your speech some material of special interest
  to them – the place, the date or a local person.
  A little humour here can be good, if it is
  introduced in the right way. (More about trying to be funny later.)

- *Present yourself.* The audience is sizing you
  up. Be honest and kind. Establish a friendly
  and receptive attitude.

- *Announce your topic.* Create immediate audience anticipation. State your main idea,
  clearly and concisely. Do it in a way to arouse

interest. Do not tell the title of your speech if the chairperson has already done so. Try memorizing this part of your introduction.

The main body

This is where you deliver the 'goods'. It is the substance of your speech. You develop the theme using facts, examples and illustrations. You continually proceed towards your predetermined conclusion.

There are four general intentions of the body.

1. *To persuade.* This is usually emphasized at a sales meeting.

2. *To instruct.* This is usually the easiest – provided you know your subject.

3. *To inspire.* You do this at an employee meeting to reduce absenteeism.

4. *To entertain.* Here you try to be funny. You may think this is the easiest. It's not. Some speakers have never found that out.

The outline

Prepare a plan for the main body – a topical outline.

●   It will help you say what you want to say. Knowing is not the same as telling.

●   It will give continuity and coherence to your

speech. This will increase both interest and comprehension by the audience.

Here are some types of outlines:

● *Chronological.* Develop the outline around a chronological series of events.

● *What – how?* Outline by answering 'what, why, who, where, when and how?'. The introduction may be the appropriate place to present the what and why.

● *Cause and effect.* This may be effectively used when you present consequences of several alternative actions.

● *Others.* You may use combinations of these types. Don't let your outline become complicated. Keep it straightforward, simple and logical.

There are many ways to prepare an outline. Here is a suggestion:

1. Write all the points you want to make on 3 × 5 in. cards – a single point on each card. Carry some cards with you and jot down an idea whenever it comes to mind. This can take several days.

2. Sort the cards into piles of closely-related cards.

3.   Arrange the piles into a logical sequence.

4.   Within each pile arrange the cards in a logical and understandable order.

5.   This is your outline. You can add, delete, change or re-arrange.

Conclusion

Here is where you clinch the purpose of the speech. You 'nail it down' so the audience remembers the main idea. Do it in a climactic and memorable way. This will be the part of the speech most remembered.

It is a high achievement to prepare and deliver a speech that is progressively more intense from beginning to end. Don't blow your chance.

Here are some suggestions:

- *Choose your words carefully.* Use them concisely and dramatically to express the important idea the way you want to.

- *Avoid summation.* Do not merely repeat what you have said before.

- *Be brief.* Don't ramble.

- *Memorize it.* Memorize your conclusion. Make it short. You can do it. Say it exactly the way you want to.

- *'Thank you'*. Some speakers believe it is inappropriate to thank the audience at the close of the speech. Do it if you want to. There is nothing wrong with a sincere 'thank you' – anytime, anywhere.

Writing in out

There are two schools of thought about this. One is to write only a topical outline. Get it exactly the way you want it. Become extremely familiar with it, down to the most detailed subheadline. Then, when you speak, refer to only the main headings for guidance – from either memory or notes.

The other is to prepare a complete manuscript. If you are an inexperienced speaker it is the sure-fire way. It is also a good way to keep improving.

Here are some suggestions on writing your speech:

- *Stick to your outline*. It will make writing easier.

- *Say what you want to say*. Choose words to accurately express your thoughts.

- *Liven up your talk*. You may want to insert some anecdotes, illustrations or humour to liven up your talk. They should be relevant. Here is where some quotation dictionaries and a good filing system will be handy.

- *Keep it simple.* You do not have to use long words or complex phrases to communicate. Read Shakespeare or the Bible to check this out.

- *Avoid jargon.* Use words in the English language. Don't try to be clever.

- *No pretense.* Do not exaggerate. Be yourself.

Edit ruthlessly

When you are all done, put your written speech aside for a few days. Then pick it up and read it. You will be surprised at how dull some of your 'gems' will look.

If any word, phrase, sentence or paragraph does not illuminate your speech, take it out. If there is any doubt – remove it. We all have problems wanting to say it all. When was the last time you heard anyone complaining about a speech being too short?

10

Jokes and other stories

Jests that slap the face are not good jests (Cervantes)

Humour can be the seasoning for your speech. Jokes and humorous stories, epigrams and witty comments or definitions can add clarity and emphasis. They can be the salt and pepper – putting zest and variety into your speech. Carefully sprinkled, they add a flavour and refreshment.

There is a time for everything. Not all speeches need jokes or witty comments. Many inexperienced – and experienced – speakers mistakenly believe they must always begin with a funny story. They have the erroneous belief that funny things are frequently needed to keep the attention of the audience.

Abraham Lincoln frequently used humour in conversation. It was always kind. He rarely used it in a
public speech. Re-read the Gettysburg Address.
King Solomon, whose name is synonymous with
wisdom, counselled us: 'there is a time to weep and
a time to laugh'.

Humour and wit are not substitutes for preparation. Do not plan your speech around jokes and
examples. Carefully prepare your topical outline.
Then, while you are writing your speech, insert
well-chosen, humorous remarks in selected places.
They should be short and relevant to the subject
matter. Make your humour, wit and examples support the topical outline.

Use of jokes and humorous stories is often
abused. Here are ways to avoid this mistake:

- *Don't be cruel.* Do not hurt anyone. Stay away
  from jokes about race, ethnic minorities,
  religion, mothers-in-law, stuttering, drunks,
  etc. This type of humour is bound to be
  decidedly unfunny to someone in the audience.

- *Be the 'fall guy'.* If the joke does sting, make it
  sting yourself. When telling jokes or witty
  comments, it is easier – and better – to have
  the audience laugh at you than with you.

- *Avoid bad taste.* I should not even have to say
  anything about this, but many speakers seem
  unable to resist telling an off-colour joke. It

appeals to their vanity. An off-colour joke will always bring a few chuckles – it's a sure thing. But you'll lose something – some respect. It's not worth the price! Don't do it – ever!

11

Visual aids

Seeing is believing. (Old English proverb)

They are often called 'visuals'. A more accurate terminology is 'visual aids'. Their purpose is to help the audience understand the spoken word. That's all. Because many speakers don't fully realize this, visual aids often are carelessly prepared and improperly used.

Let us discuss how to prepare and use them. We will not consider such aids as blackboards, flannelboards or flip-charts, which are often used when the speech is an informal presentation involving audience participation.

Projectors

We are considering only single-frame, still projection on to a screen remote from the projector.

Opaque projectors

These are constructed to directly project pages from a book or report. There are not many of these monstrosities around anymore. They have very poor optical qualities and they make a great amount of noise.

Overhead projectors

These project a transparency, about 8×10 in. Successive transparencies can be overlaid to illustrate a sequence of events. While a transparency is projected you may write on it with a grease pencil. Nice features! But it's all downhill from there.

These rather cumbersome machines must be located at the front of the room – between the audience and the screen. They also make considerable noise and emit stray light to annoy and distract the audience. It is virtually impossible to locate the lens perpendicular to the screen. Consequently, these machines project a distorted, 'keystone' image.

35-mm slide projectors

This equipment is now practically universal. It is

available at nearly all auditoriums, meeting centres and other speaking facilities. Mounted slides of standard size are held in high-capacity cartridges compatible with projectors representing a wide variety of manufacturers and models.

These projectors are usually equipped with a remote advance/reverse control conveniently operated by the speaker. Optical qualities are excellent. Lenses of various focal length are available, permitting the projector to be located at the back of the room or in a projection booth. A dissolve unit may be operated with two projectors, enabling smooth transition between successive slides.

How to prepare slides

Here are some suggestions for preparing material to be photographed:

- Don't make the slide if it does not explain the subject better than words.

- Generally use the horizontal format – about 5 in. horizontal to $3\frac{1}{2}$ in. vertical.

- Don't use vertical printing.

- Keep charts and graphs simple. Show only highlights.

- Use the simplest terms – only key words or phrases.

- Use only one idea on each slide.

- Use no more than 40 characters horizontally per line – including spaces.

- Use no more than eight horizontal lines.

- Use no more than four curves per graph. No date points.

- If possible, use an identical chart layout for all slides in the presentation.

- Use neat draftsmanship.

- Throw away all poorly exposed or un-focused slides.

How to use visual aids

It's a team – you and the equipment. Let's talk about the equipment first.

Here are things to do before your speech begins:

- Check the length of the extension cords. Do they fit the outlets?

- Be sure the projector works, is set up properly and the lens is focused.

- Is there a spare bulb? Does anybody know how to change it and remove a stuck slide?

- If there is a projectionist, work out a 'slide advance' signal.

- If there is a speaker's control, become familiar with it.

- Check your slides. Do you have the right ones? Are they in proper sequence and position? Do they advance without sticking?

- Assign someone to control room lights. If lights cannot be dimmed, leave some on in the back of the room.

- Check the seating. Can everyone see?

- Check the speaker's lectern for everything you will need – pointer and lapel microphone if you must move to the screen.

- Can you read your outline or notes when the lights are dimmed?

Here is a checklist about you – things to remember while you speak:

- Do not dim the lights until you actually need the slides.

- The projected slide should show only what you are currently talking about.

- Avoid intermittent use of the slides during your presentation. Arrange your speech so that all the slides are shown in an unbroken sequence.

- Look at the audience while the slides are

projected. No one is interested in the back of your head.

- Turn up the lights immediately when finished with the slides, then continue your presentation.

A word of warning

Visual aids can be tremendously useful for some occasions such as professional presentations, technical briefings, administrative reporting and a host of other instructional speeches. However, when slides are projected in a darkened room the speaker immediately becomes isolated from the audience. There is danger of losing some of the close personal relationship so essential to good public speaking.

The gain in communication efficiency by using visual aids may be more imagined than real. All speakers should carefully weigh the advantages and disadvantages.

To paraphrase the old merchandising maxim, 'Let the speaker beware!'

12

Ways to tell it

The best orator is one who can make men see
with their ears. (Arab proverb)

The essential ingredient

Now that you have prepared your speech, there are several ways you can deliver it. An essential feature of any good presentation – regardless of how you present it – is to establish and maintain a personal and cordial relationship with the audience. It's indispensable to any of the following ways.

The memorized speech

One way is to memorize it, word for word. Many

speech books, however, say to never memorize a speech – never! A very dogmatic notion; I am going to disagree with it.

Some speeches are suited to memorizing, some are not. There are pitfalls and traps, too. If you decide to memorize, be aware of them.

Here are some speeches appropriate for memorizing:

● A short speech – from four to six minutes. It's possible, of course, to memorize longer speeches. However, I suggest you stick to the short ones.

● A speech which will be repeated at other places, to different audiences.

● An especially dramatic or humorous speech – where you desire an unusually close relationship with the audience.

Keep in mind that some very bad things can happen to you while presenting a memorized speech. Your mind might go blank, or you might sing-song your way through the entire speech – no tonal variety, no voice inflection, no speech rhythm. Not very impressive (favourably, that is).

That is only two. But they are enough!

How to do it

Knowing the problems is a step towards the solution. Here are suggestions about memorizing a short speech.

1. Divide your speech into 10–15 small, logical parts – between each topic or set of closely related sentences and adjacent to illustrative material.

2. Then slightly rework the wording at the end of each part so it has a key word or phrase closely related to the general idea of the next part.

3. These key words will automatically get you started on the next part.

4. Start memorizing early. At first, concentrate only on recalling the words.

5. A few days before the speech, begin practising with proper inflection, pauses, etc.

6. Prepare a small slip of paper listing, in chronological order, the key words to successive parts of the speech. It is your hand-held 'prompter' just in case you need it. You'll feel better having the insurance. No one will even know you have it.

Reading the speech

In this way of delivering a speech there are few, if any, deviations of the spoken word from the printed manuscript. Additions, deletions or changes from the manuscript are seldom made and have minor importance. What the audience hears is, essentially, what the speaker is reading, word for word, from the manuscript.

There are occasions when reading the manuscript is an appropriate way to present a speech. Here are some:

- when the speech involves unusually important and sensitive issues requiring exact wording;

- when exact details of events, dates or policies are important;

- when advance copies of the speech have been released;

- when the speaker must adhere to a tight time schedule.

This may seem a safe way to deliver a speech. After all, what could go wrong? But often our dangers in life are where they are least expected. Here are some things that can go wrong:

- The audience may immediately sense the presence of the manuscript. A barrier goes up!

- You might present such excessive detail that you lose the audience. This commonly happens when professional papers or technical reports are involved.

- You may unconsciously begin to read in a monotone voice, without inflection or rhythm. The audience will sleep!

- You may feel a compelling need to ad lib a few unprepared remarks to break the grinding monotony. This often causes a severe case of 'foot-in-the-mouth' disease.

- You may get into the habit of using reading as a crutch, depending on it to avoid confronting the audience.

How to do it

Here are some suggestions for reading your speech.

- Reading an important speech, or parts of a speech, can lend importance to the occasion – but don't abuse it.

- Prepare the manuscript in double-spaced, large-type print. Underline key sentences. Make it easy to read.

- Read the final lectern manuscript many times. Have it almost memorized.

- Look at the audience while you speak. Glance at the manuscript only occasionally to prompt yourself or to read significant but brief details.

- Speak in a natural manner. Avoid the sleep-inducing 'reader's voice'.

- The audience will hardly know you are reading the speech if you do it right.

The extemporaneous speech

The term 'extemporaneous' is often confused with the term 'impromptu'. An extemporaneous speech is delivered according to a carefully predetermined plan. However, the speaker is so familiar with the plan that little, if any, visible reference is made to it during the presentation.

An important characteristic of extemporaneous speaking is its naturalness. It conveys the personality of the speaker to the audience. Consequently, the audience becomes more attentive and receptive. Tests have shown an audience retains about 35 per cent more from an extemporaneous speech than from any other.

The extemporaneous speech is suited to all occasions. It has universal application. With the exception of short, memorized portions from the main body, your material can usually be presented most effectively in the extemporaneous manner.

Even national government leaders – accomplished speakers – often read word for word from a teleprompter or cue cards to give the illusion of an extemporaneous speech.

Many speakers avoid extemporaneous speaking in favour of *reading* the speech, because of fear. The mere mention of speaking only from notes causes terror and trembling.

The way to conquer fear is to do the thing you fear most – and to go on doing it until you have built up a record of successful experiences.

How to do it

Here are some suggestions for speaking extemporaneously:

- Prepare a written manuscript.

- Read it over many times. Become thoroughly familiar with it.

- Prepare a speaking outline consisting of the main speech topics, including brief material you want to quote directly. Here are two ways:

  1. use standard $8\frac{1}{2} \times 11$ in. paper or, for convenience at the lectern, use 5×8 in. cards; or

  2. make a chronological list of the main topics on small, palm-held cards. You will greatly appreciate this method at those unexpected times when a speaker's lectern is unavailable.

- Memorize the main topics of the outline.

- Practise delivering the speech using the outline only as a prompter. Check to make sure you stay close to the working manuscript.

A combination of ways

Often there are occasions when memorizing and reading can be effectively combined with the extemporaneous method. Memorizing brief passages requiring the exact, predetermined wording can achieve the extemporaneous effect yet retain the preciseness of thought. Also, purposefully reading short, important passages can lend emphasis and dramatic effect to the extemporaneous speech.

The impromptu speech

The impromptu speech is presented with no predetermined detailed plan or outline. The speaking occasion arises unannounced and probably unexpectedly. It can come both off the job and at work. So, the ability to speak in the impromptu manner is a tremendous asset.

This does not imply that the capable impromptu speaker is either uninformed or unprepared. They arrive equipped with the tools of prior experience, listening, reading and thinking about the subject.

You acquire expanded knowledge and interests as you improve your ability to organize your thoughts for formal public speaking. While doing so, you can also enhance your skills for impromptu speaking.

How to do it

Get into the habit of anticipating the opportunity for the short impromptu speech or comment.

Before the occasion for the speech arises, mentally form a short plan.

1. State the main idea.

2. Develop the argument.

3. State the conclusion.

Then, when the 'unexpected' occasion does arrive, stand and concisely present the impromptu speech from your mental outline.

Do some thinking at your seat. Don't leave it all to thinking on your feet. If you have nothing to say, don't stand up.

The entertainment speech

A few words now about the humorous speech.

Here is where you entertain – only. You are not trying to inform or save souls. There is no introduction, main body or conclusion. This type of speech is unique, in a class by itself.

Mark Twain, an accomplished humorous speaker,

had a talent for stretching out one humorous incident for the duration of a highly entertaining speech. Other humorous speakers have a 'machine-gun' delivery, rapidly firing off salvos of one-liners, short jokes and witty comments about a variety of subjects. Others develop their highly humorous speech around a definite topic. There is no set pattern for a successful humorous speech.

If you do decide to give a humorous speech, here are some tips:

- Keep your first attempts short. (And remember, you'll make it without notes!)

- Select your jokes carefully.

- Arrange the anecdotes, jokes, witty comments and other narratives in an order so that one leads to the other. This will do two things:

  1. Your speech will flow in an easy and natural order.

  2. It will help you to remember what comes next.

- Practise until it all comes easily.

- Be yourself. Don't try to imitate other noted comedians.

- Be flexible. Save an unusually good story for the last. Don't hesitate to go to it sooner than usual if things aren't going right.

13

Rehearsing

Practice is everything. (Periander of Corinth, 600 BC)

More than 2,500 years later, Ralph Waldo Emerson put it in a slightly different way: 'Practice is nine-tenths.' Is practice really all that important? Yes!

Effective public speakers universally recognize the value of practising and rehearsing. It is a vital part of speech preparation.

Winston Churchill had a love affair with the English language. Few men have appreciated the value of the spoken word more or have been more skilled in its use. His colourful and dramatic career was highlighted by his zeal for writing and speaking effectively. As skilled a speaker as he later became, however, he never abandoned his self-imposed rule of carefully rehearsing every speech.

Reasons to rehearse

There are many reasons for you to rehearse the delivery of your prepared speech, including to:

1. help you detect 'bugs' in your manuscript, such as

    ● grammatical violations, poor word selection or incoherent sentence structure,

    ● illogical organization,

    ● inadequate information or excessive detail,

    ● poor logic and reasoning;

2. help you look and feel more comfortable;

3. improve your vocal variety and speech phrasing;

4. improve the effectiveness of your gestures;

5. reduce annoying mannerisms so the right words come out naturally and pleasantly;

6. avoid mispronounced words;

7. help you use your visual aids effectively;

8.   help you finish on time;

9.   stop you from any new but bad ideas.

How to do it

The first thing you need to do is to stop feeling self-conscious about rehearsing. This prevents many speakers from practising. They think they will feel 'so silly' that they avoid ever trying.

Next, you need to adopt an inflexible rule about its urgency. Repeatedly rehearse every speech.

Start early so you have the opportunity to do it many times – at least every day for the week before the speech.

Use the same words and gestures you will use at the speech. Do it exactly as you will when speaking.

Rehearse in front of a mirror. Watch yourself carefully. Or, rehearse in front of a video-camera at home. Accept any criticism graciously.

Go through the entire speech each time you rehearse. Duplicate the speaking situation as closely as possible.

Talk to the tombstones. A young aspirer once asked Benjamin Disraeli what course of study to take to become a speaker. Disraeli asked, 'Is there a graveyard near your house?' 'Yes,' was the reply. 'Then,' said Disraeli, 'I recommend you to visit it early in the mornings and practise to the tombstones.'

14

Just before it begins

You may fire when ready, Gridley. (Admiral David G. Farragut)

What you do during the last 30 minutes before the programme starts can greatly affect how your speech goes. You have worked so hard up to now in all phases of preparation, it would indeed be unfortunate to neglect these vital last few moments. Here are some tips to make everything run smoothly:

- Arrive about 30 minutes before the programme begins.

- Meet the chairperson or whomever will introduce you. Give that person a brief written statement about yourself, if you have not done so already.

- If copies of the written manuscript are available, ask the chairperson to announce it.

- Tell the chairperson if there will be a discussion after the speech.

- Have a brief and cordial conversation with others on the programme.

- Check facilities at the lectern. Stand behind it. Become familiar with it.

- If a portable lectern is to be brought in, find out about it – where will it be located?

- If a public address system is available, use it unless it is defective or the room is small.

- Use a lapel microphone, if available.

- Try out the acoustics of the room with the public address system. Pre-set the volume. Is someone assigned to adjust the controls?

- Is there water at the lectern?

- If you will be using slides, check all the things about them we have previously discussed.

- Check your appearance – how do you look?

- Find a quiet place for a few minutes of concentration on your speech.

If you leave the room, be careful where you go. Several years ago I went to a nice quiet room. Soon a woman came in. The conversation went like this:

Woman: 'Who are you?'

Me: 'I am tonight's speaker. I just came in here to think about my speech.'

Woman: 'Do you always get nervous like this?'

Me: 'Nervous? Who's nervous? I am not nervous.'

Woman: Well, if you're not nervous, what are you doing here in the ladies' cloak room?'

15

How to use your mouth and other things

Let your speech be always with grace, seasoned with salt. (Colossians, 4:6)

The audience is both listening and watching. The things they see are not in the manuscript – nor, maybe, some of the things they hear. Both are important, yet you, as the speaker, may be unaware of either their existence or their consequences.

Here are some suggestions for being favourably seen and heard:

Your general appearance

Appearance alone does not make the speaker. But it will pay to appear at your best. A good exterior is a silent recommendation – it is a premium every-where.

Dress appropriately for the occasion. Be careful about casual clothes. You will never go wrong dress-ing up.

Be neat. Shine your shoes. Comb your hair. Check your make-up. Are your clothes pressed? You get the idea!

Use good posture. Stand erect – don't slouch. Standing up straight not only looks good, but it will improve your voice.

Don't lean on the lectern. It makes you look tired, like you need a rest.

Your face

The audience will be looking at your face most of the time. Your audience receives your message from your face. Two thousand years ago the Roman poet Ovid wrote, 'A pleasing countenance is no small advantage'. (He later got run out of the country, but that's another story.)

I am going to mention two things about your face: mouth and eyes.

1. *Smile.* A cheerful face on the speaker will bring cheerful faces to the audience. It's difficult for a smiling audience to be either unattentive or disinterested.

2. *Eyes*. Look at the audience. Get into the habit of directing your attention for brief periods to all sections of the audience. If you look at them, they will look at you.

Your hands

No one has a 'hand problem' during normal conversation – we use our hands to gesture in a natural way. We are not even aware of them.

A good speaker automatically delivers a well-rehearsed speech in a manner similar to normal conversation – naturally and effortlessly. The speaker then does not regard 'hands' as a problem, but uses natural hand gestures to supplement the easy flow of speech. Rehearsing pays!

To the male speaker, I advise you purposefully to avoid putting your hands into your pockets. This may take considerable resolve. Merely having your hands in your pockets does not distract the audience, but repeatedly putting your hands in your pockets can cause a distraction.

Here are a couple of things you should never do with your hands. I wouldn't even be mentioning them if they were not such a common problem:

1. Don't pick your nose.

2. Don't scratch where it itches.

Your voice

There is a widespread need for a thorough cultivation of the voice. It is surprising how few speakers give real attention to this important subject.

Here are some suggestions on using your voice at the lectern.

- *Speak up*. No one in the audience should have to strain to hear. Nor should you have to shout.

- *Use good diction*. Enunciate your words clearly so the audience can understand. You must not slur your words or mumble. Don't try to speak while chewing gum or smoking.

- *Breathe normally*. Your sentences in ordinary conversation are short. You complete them before running out of breath. Remember that when writing your speech.

- *Speak pleasantly*. This means using pleasing tonal variety, voice inflection and speech rhythm. Your voice should sound natural, a characteristic of normal conversation. Again, rehearsing pays.

- *Improve voice quality*. Many speakers, through habit, tighten the mouth and throat muscles, causing the voice to rise to an unnatural and unpleasant higher pitch. There is a tendency to do this during momentary nervousness at the beginning of a speech. Speech therapists can help those having a persistent unpleasant pitch.

● *Don't rush.* Don't speak too fast. Most good speakers say about 100 words per minute. Remove some material if you will run overtime.

● *Is your throat dry?* Take a small sip of water when you first feel it. Bite your tongue lightly if you have no water.

Speech mannerisms

A mannerism is a habit. It's like a rope – you weave a strand each day, and soon we cannot break it.

It is just as easy to form a good habit as a bad one. Also, it is as hard to break a bad habit as a good one. The trick is to get the good ones and keep them.

There are hundreds of different speech mannerisms, some good, some bad. Both kinds are used unconsciously. But even good ones can become distasteful when used excessively. Everyone remembers the bad ones – they distract and annoy the audience.

Below is a list of negative speech mannerisms. Work on eliminating these from your repertoire.

1. *'Uh-uh-uh.'* Many speakers have an uncontrollable urge to always have a sound pouring from their mouths. Silence is

unbearable. This mannerism becomes a 'filler' before the next idea comes – or even between each sentence! This is an extremely tough one to break.

2. *'You know.'* This one is done for the same reason as 'uh'. Avoid them both.

3. *Weaving back and forth.* This is a form of nervousness, like jiggling your foot. It's extremely distracting. Soon the audience becomes worried you will fall over.

4. *Licking lips.* There are many other facial mannerisms as well: grimacing, head jerking and all the other distractive variations. When these nervous habits do not exist during ordinary conversation, better speech preparation is the sure cure.

5. *Repeated meaningless hand gestures.* Variety and spontaneity of hand gestures can lend dramatic emphasis. Some speakers limit postures to one or two repeated movements. Anticipated, unnatural and inappropriate, they become an embarrassment.

6. *Playing with things.* Toying and fiddling with handy items such as eyeglasses, pencils, keys or note cards can become a stimulating attraction to the audience. Soon they are not listening. Do not even pick things up if you can't control yourself.

16

Speaker's style

*The way of speaking I love is natural and plain –
a sinewy way of expressing one's self. It is free
from affectation. (Michel De Montaigne)*

A mannerism is specific. A speaker's style is the general way of selecting, using, expressing and emphasizing words. It is distinct from the idea of the speech.

We often regard style in terms of a current fashion. Not so for style in public speaking. Here it has a more lasting quality, a permanence. It is often the characteristic or quality most identified with the speaker.

The speaker's personality

The speaker's personality is reflected in the style of delivery. You cannot mask your personality from your speaking style. Eventually, your personality will be revealed. This gives a clue on how to develop an effective and pleasing style of speaking.

The 'right' style

There is no single correct style. Styles vary widely among successful speakers. Here are examples of accomplished speakers having widely differing styles. In each case the style reflects a measure of the character of the speaker.

- *Accessibility.* Charles de Gaulle, the French national leader, at all times maintained a style of regal aloofness from his audience and devoted following. President Harry Truman, on the other hand, spoke with extreme candour and frankness.

- *Speed.* A characteristic of the Reverend Billy Graham's effective style is a rapid speaking rate, conveying a sense of urgency to his message. Other speakers emphasize what they have to say by adopting a very deliberate, exact style.

- *Word selection.* William Jennings Bryan, the 'man with the golden tongue', had a style of flamboyant expression using colourful phrases and unusual similes. Abraham Lincoln invariably conveyed his ideas with well-chosen, unadorned, simple words.

- *Humility.* A distinguished feature of Booker T. Washington was extreme modesty and humility. The style of General Douglas MacArthur emphasized confidence and assurance to such an extent that humility was unnoticed.

An art to learn

This is the first time I have used the word 'art'. Often art is regarded as an inherent, not an acquired talent. For some forms of art this is true. Speaking style is an art, but it can be developed. Here are some thoughts about developing a pleasant speaking style.

- *Enduring ideas.* Your style should be the way you can do the most. Forget about immediate rewards. Lincoln's debates with Douglas did not get him a seat in the US Senate, but he is now remembered for greater goals. Both Hitler and Mussolini had a dynamic speaking style – but they didn't last. Become interested and involved in enduring ideas and values.

- *Sincerity.* Effective speech must come from one's convictions. Nothing replaces sincerity. Will Rogers was one of America's most beloved humorists. A sincere funny guy? He loved people and he meant it when he said, 'I never met a man I didn't like'. His audience understood.

- *Enthusiasm.* Become genuinely interested in what you talk about. Ralph Nader, an effective speaker, violates many 'rules' of speaking. He walks to the lectern carrying an outlandish armload of books, rolled-up newspapers and reports to support his ideas. He is always enthusiastic about his urgent message; enthusiasm can't be turned on and off like a faucet.

- *Be yourself.* You are free to use any style, provided it is natural, sincere and effective. But you must be yourself. Be honest, loving and sympathetic. You should never appear clever and make a show of your talents. Applause will come unsolicited from those who know what to applaud.

  Don't try to be someone else, adopting a style you admire. Develop your own style.

- *Improve yourself.* Don't remain the same person tomorrow as you are today. Discover where your shortcomings are. Continually repair them. Study other speakers. Use the good points that fit the person you want to be. Improve yourself – improve your style.

17

Is anyone listening?

The chief fault with audiences is they often see the point before you get there. It is disconcerting. (J. K. Jerome)

Occasionally a speaker may see unmistakable signs of audience disinterest and inattention. If it is widespread the audience probably has justifiable complaints, such as:

- the speech is disorganized and hard to follow;

- they cannot hear because the speaker is talking too fast;

- it's boring;

- the speaker is not interested in it, either;

- it's too long.

These are sure signs of poor speech preparation. There is little a speaker can do in the middle of a speech to correct this neglect. Impromptu remarks and off-the-cuff comments usually increase the trouble. The best immediate solution is to quickly wind it up and sit down.

Use this experience to learn a most valuable lesson about the importance of speech preparation.

The unexpected disturbance

Sometimes when you are delivering a well-prepared speech to an interested and appreciative audience, an unexpected disturbance may occur. The extent of distraction to the audience depends on the persistence of the disturbance and how the speaker handles it.

Several types of disturbances, although unplanned, are rather common. Their destructive consequences can be reduced if the speaker has a general, predetermined policy for handling them. The unexpected disturbance is then no longer a surprise.

There is no single correct way to handle each type. Details of each situation vary. Also, the appropriate way to handle them will depend upon the personality and style of the speaker.

My recommendations for handling these common,

unexpected disturbances reflect my style. I offer some general rules:

- Don't hurt anyone. Be kind.

- Make the joke on yourself when you use humour to smooth things over.

- Resist the urge to put someone down.

There are countless distracting surprises that can come unannounced. Here are my suggestions for some of them:

- *The unfriendly audience.* You may face an unfriendly audience. This may be a surprise or you may have anticipated it. Either way, your best approach is to emphasize points of agreement. Never become argumentative. You will not convert anyone.

- *People leaving.* Some of the audience may come in late, move around or leave early. Ignore them if they are small in number. Don't admonish anyone. Terminate your speech early if the situation becomes a mass exodus.

- *Crying babies.* It is a born instinct. Don't get all uptight. You can ease the embarrassment of the parents if, during your introduction, you graciously announce they may leave and return. Make them feel welcome.

- *Photographers.* They will be down in front between you and the audience. All they want is a picture of you 'in action' – mouth open with an outstretched arm. Help them. Hold the pose momentarily during your normal speech delivery. Then they will be gone.

- *Pause – a long one.* Sometimes, in spite of all your preparation, memory momentarily fails. It may seem like eternity. It's not. Here is where a little humour on yourself can turn a 'disaster' into an asset. For example, tell them your biggest mistake tonight was when you got up out of your chair. You will have time to remember what to say while they are laughing. There are jokes you can tell on yourself to cover any situation.

- *The drunk.* If there is a social hour before the programme, you may encounter people who have had too much to drink. If you think there will be a problem, politely mention this to the chairperson or toastmaster. Let someone else handle this potential source of trouble. Never compete from the lectern with a drunk.

- *The heckler.* You hear a lot about hecklers. They are not as prevalent as you might think. If you ever have this problem, never respond to the taunts. Stay cool. Keep poised. If it persists, calmly sit down.

● *Mistakes*. Even accomplished speakers make mistakes. Things like a mispronounced word, forgetting a name, using the wrong name, notes falling off the lectern, slides upside down – the possibilities are endless. Have a repertoire of humorous comments and stories specifically appropriate for several common, unplanned situations. The spontaneity of these remarks can be a highlight of your speech.

The ability to maintain flexibility in your speech does not imply any relaxation of thorough preparation. Flexibility is an added dimension of preparation – be prepared to be flexible.

The ability to smoothly modify, delete or add material to a well-prepared speech while at the lectern is a skill achieved with experience ... and no small amount of planning and preparation.

18

Questions and answers

Men are never so likely to settle a question rightly as when they discuss it freely. (T. B. Macaulay)

To have or have not

Questions after a formal presentation are evidence of an attentive audience. A question-and-answer period can contribute to the speech, clarifying and expanding points of special interest to the audience.

Some speakers like to have a question-and-answer period. The decision to accept questions is up to the speaker. It is important to be so thoroughly informed that you can handle any question on the subject. An important ingredient of being informed is to know what is not known.

How to do it

If you, as a speaker, do decide to answer questions, here are some suggestions:

1. Notify the chairperson about your decision before the speech.

2. Have the chairperson announce after the conclusion of your speech that you will answer questions.

The question-and-answer format will depend on the size of the audience.

If the room is so small it doesn't require a public address system, invite the questioner to stand and directly ask you the question. Politely stress the need for brevity. Repeat the question to ensure that all heard.

If it's a large audience, suggest to the chairperson that questions be written on paper furnished by ushers after you have finished. These are to be quickly collected and given to the chairperson who will sort them and state selected, representative questions.

Then, state the answer concisely and briefly.

Don't argue with a contentious questioner – it's not a debate. If they persist, politely list points of agreement and move on.

If you do not know the answer, say so. Offer to meet the questioner afterwards to obtain their name and address for replying later.

Terminate the session if the hour is getting late, even if the discussion is lively and enthusiastic. Some people will be wanting to go home. Announce that you will remain afterwards to continue the discussion.

19

After it's all done

All over but the shouting. (Popular saying)

All done. The speech is delivered! Here's what happens now. You will soon receive a letter from the chairperson. It will be a thank-you letter, kindly expressing appreciation for the speech. A nice gesture. Another nice gesture would be to mail a reply. Nothing fancy, just a short, sincere acknowledgment of their thanks is always in style.

Evaluate the speech

We hear much about the value of experience. It is often regarded as the ultimate standard for qualification. But experience has no standard. Ten years of experience might be merely one year's experience repeated ten times. The first thing we need to do is identify our mistakes.

You probably have a pretty good idea of how your speech went. However, we are frequently deceived by our own thoughts about ourselves. Here are some suggestions about asking, receiving and using criticism.

- Get opinions from others who heard the speech. Do it soon afterwards while it is still fresh in their minds.

- Ask people whose judgement you regard highly and who will freely offer candid criticism.

- Ask for criticism on all aspects of the presentation, that is: appropriateness of topic, comprehensiveness of material, clarity of organization and delivery.

- Take all comments in a receptive and gracious manner. Never question their validity.

- Later, evaluate the criticism. Do it honestly and objectively.

- Incorporate corrective action into future speeches. Don't keep making the same mistakes. Be determined to improve with each successive speech.

21

Bon voyage

I travel not to arrive – but to go. I travel for travel's sake.
The great affair is to move. (R. L. Stevenson)

I have three hopes.

First, I hope you have enjoyed reading this book about public speaking as much as I have enjoyed writing it. It has been a joy.

I also hope it has been informative.

Thirdly, I hope that while you improve your speaking skills, you have a pleasant journey along the way. May your 'great affair' also be to move.

Someone once asked Winston Churchill how to end a speech. He replied, 'When you have said all you have to say, and come to a sentence with a grammatical ending – sit down.'

I think my time has come.

Index

Brain Sell

Tony Buzan and Richard Israel

All selling is a brain-to-brain process, in which the salesperson's brain communicates with the customer's. Recent new discoveries in the fields of psychology, communication, general science, sports and Olympic training techniques, neurophysiology, brain research, sales research and selling techniques have resulted in *Brain Sell*. In this remarkable book the world's leading expert on harnessing the power of the brain joins forces with a pioneer of modern sales training to show how you can become a high sales producer.

Brain Sell, based on the latest scientific research and the experiences of some of the world's most successful salespeople, explains how to:

• identify which mental skills are currently being used in selling
• apply whole brain selling to any sales situation
• use a multi-sensory format in selling
• develop your sales memory and remember customers' names and faces
• Mind Map and be prepared for the 'sales information age'
• master the mind-body link
• keep focused and retain customer information
• mentally rehearse the sale
• make memorable sales presentations
• develop and use a personal sales commercial.

All of this, together with over 80 skill-building exercises, guarantee a multitude of new ideas in *Brain Sell* for everyone who sells - whatever the type of product or service, and whether you're a beginner or a veteran. Try it!

Gower

How to Negotiate Worldwide
A Practical Handbook

Donald W Hendon and Rebecca Angeles Hendon

As the world continues to shrink, the ability to operate on a global scale is becoming a necessity for more and more business people. And the rewards of knowing how to negotiate in different markets can be enormous.

This book is based on the experience of thousands of managers who have attended the seminars run by the authors in more than twenty countries. From it you will learn: how changing conditions in international business are affecting the way people negotiate; the distinct stages of negotiation; the price concession patterns preferred by executives from fifteen different countries; how to observe, interpret and use non-verbal behaviour across a range of cultures; the seventy-three favourite tactics chosen by executives from eleven countries - and how to counter them.

With anecdotes, case studies, exercises, checklists and a cultural self-awareness questionnaire, here is a book that actively involves the reader. If you are one of the increasing number of managers who expect to deal with, work with, or live among members of different cultures, then this book is for you.

Gower

How to Organize a Conference

Iain Maitland

Next to making a presentation, organizing a conference is probably the task most likely to induce panic in even the most competent of managers. So many details to attend to! So many things to go wrong! And all of it taking place in public!

But help is at hand. Using a unique blend of questions, checklists and illustrative documents, Iain Maitland's book will guide you through the minefield. With its aid you will find yourself planning, promoting and staging a successful event - and remembering to evaluate it afterwards so that the next one will be even better.

From this book you will learn how to: • set appropriate objectives • establish a sensible budget - and adhere to it • draft an appealing programme • plan a realistic schedule • choose a suitable venue • publicize the event • speak well in public • use equipment to best advantage • stage rehearsals • manage the event itself • follow through and much more besides.

The fourteen chapters cover in detail every aspect of conference organizing, and are supported by a reference section giving details of useful tools and contacts. At the end is a comprehensive checklist indexed to the text, providing both a complete summary and a way of looking back at any particular item. It may be possible to run a successful conference without Iain Maitland's book - but why take that risk?

Gower

How to Write Effective Reports

2nd Edition

John Sussams

In business, administration and research, the report is an indispensable tool and all managers or specialists need to master the skills involved in writing one. John Sussams' book covers all aspects of the subject in a thoroughly practical fashion. It not only discusses language and style but also explains how to structure and organize material to facilitate understanding. In addition it deals with planning, presentation and production.

The text is enlivened by examples and illustrations and there are a number of exercises designed to improve the reader's report-writing ability.

Gower

Project Leadership

2nd Edition

Wendy Briner, Colin Hastings and Michael Geddes

The bestselling first edition of this book broke new ground by focusing on the leadership aspects of project management rather than the technical. This radically revised edition is substantially reorganized, to introduce much new material and experience and bring the applications up to date.

Project leaders now exist in many different types of organizations, and they and their projects extend far wider than the construction work where traditional project management began. This new edition begins by explaining why the project way of working has been so widely and enthusiastically adopted, and provides new material on the role and key competences of project leaders in a wide range of different organizations. The authors provide invaluable guidance to senior managers struggling to create the context within which project work can thrive as well as be controlled. A new section, 'Preparing the Ground' reflects their increased emphasis on getting projects off to the right start, with new insights into the scoping process designed to ensure all parties agree on objectives. It also demonstrates the importance of understanding the organizational and political factors involved if the project is to succeed in business terms.

Part III shows how to handle the issues that arise at each stage of the project's life including a whole new section on the critical process of project team start up. The final section contains a thought-provoking "action summary" and a guide to further sources of information and development.

Project leadership and the project way of working has moved on. This book will provide both a conceptual framework and a set of practical tools for all those who find themselves permanently or occasionally in the project leader role, as well as an invaluable guide to setting up and maintaining project activity.

Gower